Maikol Nascimento Pinto

Social Entrepreneurship & Network Management

AF154759

Maikol Nascimento Pinto

Social Entrepreneurship & Network Management

Incubation and Development

ScienciaScripts

Imprint

Any brand names and product names mentioned in this book are subject to trademark, brand or patent protection and are trademarks or registered trademarks of their respective holders. The use of brand names, product names, common names, trade names, product descriptions etc. even without a particular marking in this work is in no way to be construed to mean that such names may be regarded as unrestricted in respect of trademark and brand protection legislation and could thus be used by anyone.

Cover image: www.ingimage.com

This book is a translation from the original published under ISBN 978-613-9-61544-5.

Publisher:
Sciencia Scripts
is a trademark of
Dodo Books Indian Ocean Ltd. and OmniScriptum S.R.L publishing group

120 High Road, East Finchley, London, N2 9ED, United Kingdom
Str. Armeneasca 28/1, office 1, Chisinau MD-2012, Republic of Moldova, Europe
Printed at: see last page
ISBN: 978-620-7-23475-2

To all those who believe in collective social development from a critical perspective.

ACKNOWLEDGMENTS

To the Great Architect of the Universe, the inexhaustible source of joy, inspiration and meaning in life. I have reached this point with a sense of "mission accomplished", strong enough to continue on my journey, but grateful and sensitive enough to recognize that it was He who fulfilled one of my heart's greatest desires: to contribute to *society*.

To my parents, Maria and Celio, examples of courage and renunciation, who contributed to my ethical upbringing, taught me to be passionate about studying and made me aware that knowledge, apart from being taken by force, is worthwhile, but requires a lot of effort, dedication and renunciation.

To my beloved partner Leandro, who, with his contagious happiness, was with me every step of the way as I carried out this work.

To my siblings and friends, who understood that I often had to be absent.

The Father Leo Commissari Association and the Solidarity Economic Enterprises in its social network, for cooperating in making this research possible.

"Time is your capital; you have to know how to use it.
Wasting time and ruining life"
Franz Kafka

This study aims to discuss how the process of social management and development takes place through social networks, to verify the interests that led entrepreneurs to seek out the solidarity economy incubator of the Padre Leo Commissari Association to start their companies and to identify the role of the network in the development of the incubated companies. The qualitative research used secondary data to characterize the neighbourhood in which the social incubator is located, and primary data from two companies linked to it. The information collected and analyzed made it possible to verify the entrepreneurs' perceptions of the incubator and to find out, from their perspective, whether being part of the social network has changed their lives. The theoretical framework of social management, development and social networks also made it possible to verify the entrepreneurs' perceptions of the incubator and the social network they are part of. Finally, we observed some aspects related to learning and administrative management, the continuity and strengthening of the incubated ventures towards self-management, as well as the promotion of economic growth that a social incubator can bring about, by providing greater entrepreneurial opportunities for the underprivileged population, in the creation of their own companies.

Keywords: Social Entrepreneurship; Development; Incubation; Social Networks; Solidarity Economy.

SUMMARY

INTRODUCTION

Social management has been considered a field of knowledge in recent years. Because it indicates new ways of organizing socio-productive practices in order to achieve development and, considering its social representativeness, it has aroused the interest of researchers from various fields.

The analysis of social dynamics, interrelated to the actions of citizens in society and public policies, contributes to the discussion of the process of transforming society, so that social management plays a role in promoting social change.

According to Junqueira (2008), there is no way of approaching social management without referring to the management of public social actions, i.e. the demands and rights of citizens, which has become an important issue within the economy, so that its potential contributes increasingly to the national GDP, generating jobs, qualifying the public debate and determining new forms in the cycle of public policies, especially social and environmental ones.

In order to respond to the demand for their rights to be met, decentralized and citizen-participatory management can be considered part of the social management trend, so that these citizens collaborate effectively with the government in achieving development. Through citizen participation, the chances increase that the people involved in the organization of decision-making policies will feel part of the social management process and will be encouraged to take an interest in development.

The process of social management needs to take place in a relational and articulated manner, in agreement between the interests of social actors and public management. Such management has become primarily responsible for regulating the market, and has sidelined dialogue with collective actions, which have great opportunities to cooperate for social progress.

Based on this perception, this research will adopt the concept of social management as the participatory process of people in decision-making for development, collaborating with the emancipation of the citizen.

Considering that social management takes place in the public sphere, emancipation is characterized as the search for autonomy, the result of the collective positioning of people and their practices. By participating in decision-making processes, citizens become able to characterize the public sphere and contribute to social management by enhancing the social impact of governance as the actors involved discuss their projects and actions.

These actors need to be aware of collective demands so that they can contribute to development. However, the question remains as to how interactivity and cooperation between the various social actors can contribute to this progress.

People's creative efforts to generate wealth and transform the social and economic environment can unleash new products (and innovative means of production), services, markets and new forms of organization.

Linked to social management, social development will also be analyzed qualitatively in this research from the perspective of the result of interrelated actions that make it possible to promote social change.

For Fernandes (1960), "development", from a social perspective, is understood as

> an inclusive concept, which encompasses all the phenomena of change that occur through the structural differentiation and functional reintegration of complete global social systems, considered in particular conditions of time and space (Fernandes, 1960, p. 12).

For the author, development is the result of various interrelated actions and phenomena in a process between social actors positioned in their own space and time. From this perspective, it is possible to break away from the subjection and fixity of underdevelopment, promoting social change in peripheral locations.

In this research, development is considered to be the set of skills of citizens who seek to coordinate their efforts to reduce poverty and, according to Franco (2002), achieve minimum conditions for enjoying health services, education, leisure,

7

culture, security, housing conditions and income. Thus, development is linked to sustainability, because, for Sachs (1997), sustainability, from a social perspective, is related to the process that leads to stable growth, with equitable distribution of income, generating an improvement in people's living conditions and, consequently, a reduction in the current differences in social levels.

The construction of a new social reality involves the establishment of social networks configured in an innovative way, i.e. with the participation of citizens, by providing opportunities for interdependence with political structures and, at the same time, active expression of the actors in social management decisions.

The active expression of actors in social management suggests action to bring about change and progress. In this way, these individuals can, connected in intersectoral social networks, act in the process of implementing effective social policies, around income-generating activities, and be agents of social change.

Among the actions that can promote such changes are those of social entrepreneurship. The profits from social entrepreneurship actions should be reinvested in the enterprises and/or in the consumer population, duly connected through lakes formed between the individuals involved in the social management process (Fischer, 2013; Yunus, 2008).

With regard to social ties, Granovetter (1973) outlines two types of lakes for connecting individuals. The first is the strong, closer lake, detected in more integrated, cohesive and united social groupings, able to act in solidarity with reliability in times of need. The second is the weak, casual and distant lake - typical of fragmented, permeable social constructs. And watch out:

> Individuals with few weak lakes would be deprived of information from distant parts of the social system and, as such, confined to the news and provincial views of their closest friends (GRANOVETTER, 1973, p. 1368).

The relevance of this research lies in the proposal to analyze social management from the point of view of participation, where partners, properly connected synergistically in solidarity economy networks, are able to spread the multiplier effects of business incubation, aiming at development and social change, which can be seen in the increase in their income.

The aim of this study is to discuss how the process of social management and development takes place on the basis of the social networks set up by people, as well as the reasons why entrepreneurs sought out the incubator.

A case study was carried out at the Padre Leo Commissari Association and two companies it incubates. The Association was chosen because it is an incubator for social enterprises, in which players who realize their potential to achieve development through social participation participate.

To achieve the above objective, the following specific objectives were defined:

• verify the interests that moved the entrepreneurs to seek out the incubator to start their companies;

• to identify the role of the network in the development of incubated companies, from the perspective of the interviewees.

This research therefore aims to analyze the levels of participation in social structures that can positively affect people's living conditions through social initiatives and partnerships.

This research will be organized as follows: introduction, theoretical framework, a chapter describing the Padre Leo Commissari Association and its regional context, the research results, final considerations, references and appendices.

In order to better contextualize the study, the Theoretical Framework chapter reviews the conceptual aspects considered necessary in relation to *social management, development* and *social networks*.

1 THEORETICAL FRAMEWORK

The concept of social management has been discussed in Brazil since 1990, in theoretical and practical opposition to the belief that the social and economic problems of the so-called "underdeveloped countries" would be overcome as they adjusted to the determinations of the stages of development determined by the developed countries, removing their conditions of "backwardness".

There was a belief that the *underdeveloped* countries would adjust to the demands of the developed countries and that, based on the production and accumulation of intensely predetermined and predictable production processes, wealth would automatically be redistributed among the poorest sections of the population.

Five years before the concept of social management began to be discussed in Brazil, Birley (1985) stated that, when creating organizations, or during their development, people can access their networks, with a view to entrepreneurship as a way of generating wealth and achieving development.

Thus, the entrepreneurial process develops in a network, and isolated actions tend to lose ground to collective social relationships, connected by webs of relationships capable of generating reciprocal benefits for the people involved in the network.

1.1 Social Management

According to Offredi (2013), the concept of social management hardly exists in France and, in general, in Europe itself. The closest definition of social management, for the author, is a set of "professional practices and management sciences whose object of analysis is social public policies".

Carvalho (2013), in agreement with Offredi (2013), understands social management as a concept based on a *social rule of law,* in which all citizens have their constitutional rights guaranteed. However, the core of the discussion in this paper is based on the participation of civil society in decisions of public interest, as a function of social management.

With regard to society, Franpa Filho (2013) postulates that

> [...] it is important to point out that Social Management involves the mobilization of economic resources. However, the notion of what is economic in Social Management seems to be redefined, since the means and ways of mobilizing resources, in other words, of making savings in Social Management [...] seems to resignify the very concept of what is economic, which is broadened in such a way that it seems to involve what has not been seen as economic. (FRANQA FILHO, 2013, p. 108)

Based on Franpa Filho's (2013) postulate, while social management "demands the mobilization of economic resources", there needs to be a re-signification of meanings related to economic processes, with a view to social policies. In dialogue with citizens, the needs for access, expansion and/or improvement of public education, health and transportation services, for example, can be put on the agenda and aligned with the government budget, so that all citizens have their constitutional rights guaranteed through social participation.

Thus, social management is exercised by society and indicates new forms of multi-stakeholder participation at the service of decision-making processes for collective support in the local sphere. This place marks the social context in which people, imbued with common interests, organize themselves around an activity, such as entrepreneurial activity. For Fischer (2002), social management is characterized by its collective and participatory nature, whose contours are outlined in social processes, power relations, conflicts and learning. Thus, this concept is understood as the participatory process of people in administrative decision-making for transformation, i.e. development.

There are aspects that lead to transformations in development and can be considered as ways of contributing to and expanding discussions on social management, among them the studies on citizen participation by Tenorio (2013), which are justified by six categories of analysis. The first, *discussion processes,* is essential to decision-making processes in the public sphere. The second, *inclusion, is* perceived as the scenario that provides social actors with an opening to speak, valuing and accepting them as citizens. The third, *pluralism,* focuses on the decentralization of powers - identifying the social actors who decide on a given agenda. The fourth, *participatory equality,* seeks to guarantee the same power for social actors to act constantly in the decision-making process. The fifth category, *autonomy,* is justified by the resourcefulness of communities in solving local problems. The last category proposed by Tenorio (2013) refers to the *common good,* related to the tangible and intangible benefits that are reflected in improvements in the living conditions of the communities analyzed.

Carvalho (1999) takes a different view to Tenorio (2013). For her, there is a clear perception that social actors are jointly responsible for implementing decisions and responding to social needs. It is not a question of the state losing its central role in social management, or its responsibility for guaranteeing the provision of goods and services that are citizens' rights; what is changing is the way in which this responsibility is processed.

Thus, social management comes to be understood as the management of public social actions aimed at the well-being of society in communities, not only carried out by the State, but also by civil society, private initiative or partnerships between the three sectors: State, private initiative and social organizations (CARVALHO, 1999; DOWBOR, 1999).

For Raichelis (2006), one of the great challenges is to organize social support by building a work agenda that is articulated with technical, political and ethical dimensions, in which projects take place on an ongoing basis, towards the effective exercise of people's participation in public spaces. Such participation refers to the intersection between people, referring to their objectives and values, and social capital is defined by the relationships that enable cooperation within or between different social groups (JUNQUEIRA 2000, p. 39). Therefore, once again, Raichelis (1998, p. 26) realizes that, through the action and discourse of social subjects, a set of issues can be established that concern collective destiny.

From the 1970s onwards, the inefficiency of the public sector in social affairs was noted. The centralizing and welfare role of the state was greatly eroded due to its bureaucracy and inability to meet the growing demand of the population, which needed some kind of economic aid.

With the advent of globalization, Galbraith (2004) recognizes that modern companies have become central factors in the modern economy, playing an extremely useful role in contemporary economic life, more so than previous capitalist, primitive and exploitative entities. Thus, the degradation of the welfare state gives rise to discussion of the role of large companies in overcoming poverty and meeting the essential needs of people and society.

Porter and Kramer (2002) and (2006) state that when companies use concepts such as *moral duty* and *sustainability, they* use a generic logic that is disconnected from their business strategy and operations. Yunus (2008) adds that, because of the nature of companies, they are not equipped to deal with social problems, even less to the extent that they are today, since companies are governed by orthodox free market economic thinking of maximizing profit and not just maintaining it.

According to Peyrefitte (1999), companies have always been expected, as the central institutions of society, coming from the traditional agrarian society, to participate effectively with the aim of development and a social mission, where the economic and the social are inseparable.

Yunus (2008) defines a social enterprise as one that is designed to meet a social goal, where the owners can receive their investments back after a period of time, but the profits remain in the company and are used to finance its expansion and not to pay dividends, as the social enterprise does not generate losses or dividends.

Social management is participatory, and it is up to the players to discuss their projects and future support in the public sphere, as a community and collectively, committed to a positive social impact on the solidarity economy network, on the road to development.

1.2 Development

Development is the dynamic process of stimulating social change. Related to social management and networks, the results of trusting cooperation between social actors is the empowerment of their organizational and participatory capacity, i.e. the power of these individuals to act for their own strengthening and development. This empowerment, in Costa's (2007) view, can be understood as the involvement of people in political and economic management, through decentralization, the passing on of responsibilities and the democratization of power.

For Fischer (2013), the Brazilian social agenda needs to treat public policies as "first class", considering social issues as a lever for development.

For Sen (1999), this term consists of the process of expanding the real freedoms that individuals enjoy, while freedoms also depend on other factors, such as social and economic provisions and civil rights.

Development, the fruit of social participation, built by society, which generates diverse territorial configurations, can be understood as the center of social relations in the territory and points to ways of achieving social change.

Alluding to this concept, Carvalho (2013) argues that social policies are sharing, giving power to citizens (empowerment), so that they can tackle inequalities, fight poverty and be socially included. According to Costa (2007), individuals start to interact better through understanding and assuming responsibilities and consequences, which can lead to greater decision-making power in the community, culminating in its development.

Globalization has altered the world's socio-economic configuration, as new national and international political discourses and practices have emerged, impacting on public policies, as Santos (2002) points out:

> Equally political is the reflection on the new forms of state that are emerging as a result of globalization, on the new political distribution between national

practices, international practices and global practices, on the new format of public policies in the face of the growing complexity of social, environmental and redistribution issues. (Santos, 2002, p. 2)

Dowbor (2001) presents his opinion on the new globalized system: [...] a system that knows how to produce, but doesn't know how to distribute, simply isn't enough. Especially if, on top of that, it throws millions out of work, dilapidates the environment and pays speculators more than producers. (DOWBOR, 2001, p. 20)

Dowbor's (2001) opinion does not consider that the interaction of people in economic dynamism can trigger a process of development, based on the potential to increase their opportunities to generate income, being responsible for improving the quality of life of those involved in a social network.

In view of the need for a system that knows how to distribute as well as produce, other forms of action and development instruments have been created according to the needs of the territory. On the other hand, Brandao (2012, p.45) says that it is necessary to investigate the positions, which he calls:
"localist", "social division of labor" and "local/endogenous development", and complete:

I believe that confronting this currently hegemonic view would involve discussing alternative proposals and dealing adequately with the articulation of all geographical scales.

Strategies of the so-called *Solidarity Economy* are some of the alternative development proposals, capable of articulating different geographical scales. They represent an intelligent production and distribution system, with cooperation and participatory public policies as its main anchors.

The concept of solidarity economy, in gestation at the turn of the last decade, signaled the need to understand initiatives that were emerging in Latin American and European countries. Today, the question posed involves its understanding as a field of practice and, especially, its relationship with public authorities (FRANCA FILHO, G.

15

C. de; et al, 2005).

According to Magro and Coutinho (2008), the term *Solidarity Economy* encompasses a variety of "actions and forms of associative production", ranging from local enterprises to broad economic and legal management plans:

> In Brazil, the practice of cooperatives has been flourishing since 1932, when the basic law of Brazilian cooperativism was enacted; however, since the 1990s, the debate around cooperative ventures has been gaining new prominence. (MAGRO E COUTINHO, 2008, p. 704)

Still in relation to the 1990s, Magro and Coutinho (2008) point out that

> This period was marked by a worsening of the economic crisis, with a sharp rise in unemployment and informal, partial and temporary jobs, as a result of the process of deindustrialization and productive restructuring, as well as the new neoliberal policies. This scenario ended up favoring the creation of strategies, such as "solidarity enterprises", which were able to promote the generation of work and income for the population excluded from the formal labor market (MAGRO; COUTINHO, 2008, p. 704).

The creation of solidarity enterprises thus becomes a strategy for generating work and income for people who are not part of the formal labor market. In this way, it is possible to see the solidarity economy through the prism of a re-signification of the meanings of economic action in society, approached as a field of practice in continuous constitution in Brazil.

According to Sampaio (2013), "the solidarity economy emerges to complement the void that the market economy is unable to fill" and on consumer relations, he continues:

> the solidarity economy consumer is the one who is dissatisfied, at least partially, with the market economy. [...] dissatisfaction stems from the

> inequalities established, both between the market and the consumer, and between the market itself, when there are dichotomies between large groups and micro and small enterprises. (SAMPAIO, C. A.C., 2013, p. 286)

According to Franpa Filho (2007):

> At this point, different forms of socio-economic and political self-organization are discussed. Some of the problems and challenges facing the field are highlighted, especially questions about their concrete possibilities in terms of their real capacity to generate sustainable territorial development and constitute an effective alternative to the predominant form of development, centered on the non-market economy. Finally, the fundamental vocation of these practices, contained in their original concept, is highlighted, exploring the idea associated with the theme of *another* economy (FRANQA FILHO; CUNHA, 2007, p. 157).

The understanding of solidarity economy practices suggests a new understanding of market logic and Polanyi (1975) understands economy as synonymous with market, as all forms of allocation of rare resources for alternative purposes.

From this perspective, it is necessary to reflect on ways of boosting enterprises governed by an alternative and profitable logic, so that their economic goals are not aggressive, but that they do not deny the market, turning to the valorization of the social contexts in which the people involved in the solidarity economy are inserted.

1.3 Social media

Castells (2000) introduces the discussion of networks as a new form of citizen participation, as they allow for the interdependence of political structures, while at the same time allowing for the active expression of individuals.

> The dominant functions are organized in their own networks in a space of flows that connects them all over the world, while at the same time fragmenting subordinate functions and people in the space of multiple places, made up of locations that are increasingly segregated and disconnected from each other. (Castells, 2000, p. 504)

Social networks deal with the interdependence of social structures and their relationships. It is necessary to understand them as a "system of nodes and links, coming to represent a set of autonomous participants, uniting ideas and resources around shared values and interests" (MARTELETO, 2004, p. 41-49).

In this sense, Junqueira (2000) complements Marteleto's discourse (2004):

> [...] in networks, collectively defined objectives bring together people and institutions that are committed to overcoming social problems in an integrated way. These networks are built between autonomous social beings who share objectives that guide their actions, respecting the autonomy and differences of each member. Hence the importance of each public organization, whether state or private, developing its knowledge in order to place it at the service of the collective interest in an integrated manner. (JUNQUEIRA, 2000, p. 39)

People and institutions willing to focus their efforts on social change need to be networked, bound by strong relational ties.

Returning to Granovetter's (1973) concept of ties, it can be seen that integrated, cohesive and united social groupings, capable of acting in solidarity with reliability in support, are *strong tie* relationships, while casual and distant relationships, typical of fragmented and permeable social constructs, are called *weak ties*.

Correa and Vale (2014) discuss Granovetter's (1973) approach and propose a reflection on the trajectory of social entrepreneurs in networks:

> [...] the gradualism in the trajectory of entrepreneurs, which thrives in

harmony with the evolution of relationship networks; the importance of past experience and the link to some trade in the formation of the entrepreneur; [...] and the interconnections between social and business relationships in the trajectories analyzed. (CORREA; VALE, 2014, p. 86)

Thus, thinkers focus on the trajectory of entrepreneurs from low-income backgrounds and their evolution in interpersonal networks. The aspects of low income are due to the total or partial inaccessibility of basic citizens' rights, such as health services, education, leisure, culture, security and housing, so that these people's incomes are insufficient to enjoy these services. The inaccessibility of basic citizens' rights, such as the impossibility of proving income or residence, means exclusion from various situations, such as public and banking services or benefits, searching for formal employment and buying products over the Internet.

Once entrepreneurial opportunities have been identified through trust, a network of social relationships can be established, taking into account the knowledge and skills of the people involved in the network, in order to generate income through one or more different branches of business activity.

People's creative efforts to generate wealth and transform the social and economic environment can maximize the potential for unleashing new products (and innovative means of production), services, markets and new forms of local organization if individuals are networked.

The integrated sets of projects that social entrepreneurs can create take the form of solidarity socio-economic networks; so-called *local productive arrangements,* especially in areas with low business density; and programs for sustainable development, job creation and income generation, among others (FISCHER, 2004, p. 13-41).

According to Loiola and Lagemann (2013), social networks influence the performance of incubated social enterprises and enterprises that are part of more cohesive social networks perform better. Thus, it is possible for people's creative ideas to form a solidarity economy network which, according to Franga Filho and Cunha (2009), is about an association or articulation of different solidarity economy ventures and/or initiatives with a view to creating their own circuit of economic relations and the exchange of experiences and training knowledge. The main objectives of such a network are twofold: to enable the sustainability of solidarity economy enterprises and/or initiatives in particular; and to strengthen the endogenous potential of a territory in terms of its capacity to promote its own development process. (FRANQA FILHO; CUNHA, 2009, p. 728-729)

Solidarity economy experiences need to take into account the heterogeneities and specificities of the place, associated with a process of economic growth of an endogenous nature and based on the social lakes established by individuals, thus characterizing a social network.

The social network in which social entrepreneurs can organize themselves emerges as an alternative to fighting poverty, as it puts their business projects into practice and is built on social relationships in the solidarity economy, considering that businesses are fundamental organizers of production, but recognizing that it is essential to reconsider the spaces in which they are inserted.

During the conception phase of their businesses, social entrepreneurs use their social networks or relationships to obtain resources and organizational legitimacy to enter the market. However, when these organizations join the network, they make clear the values and beliefs of their entrepreneurial practices and establish requirements that will govern the negotiations between those involved. Once the legitimization requirements have been established, the relationships and opportunities to ensure the social recognition of the organization towards improving its relationships with society are increased, so that entrepreneurship, specifically social entrepreneurship, can cooperate in this process.

In the specialized literature, there are two types of entrepreneurship: corporate (or commercial), aimed at generating financial results by exploiting (in the target public) unmet needs or desires, properly managing the human and economic resources to do so; and social entrepreneurship (recent terminology), whose commitment consists of contributing to the removal of barriers that prevent a society, or part of it, from accessing certain social markets.

Because the terminology *social entrepreneurship* is recent, Comini and Tiscosk (2014) add that

> some aspects have been imported from the corporate environment and have been the subject of debate among academics and professionals. These debates have been caused by the lack of common understanding of a new concept that tries to bring together two types of activities, considered a priori to be non-reconcilable: those aimed at doing business and those aimed at reducing negative social and environmental impacts (COMINI; ROSOLEN AND TISCOSK, 2014, p. 87).

It is important to dispel the notion that the difference between the corporate entrepreneur and the social entrepreneur can be attributed simply to motivation, with corporate entrepreneurs being driven by money and social entrepreneurs driven by altruism.

For Martin and Osberg (2007), entrepreneurs are rarely motivated by the prospect of high financial gain, as the odds of generating a lot of money are sometimes against them. Both the corporate entrepreneur and the social entrepreneur are strongly driven by the identification, pursuit and vision of the opportunity, and obtain considerable psychic reward from the process of realizing their ideas.

The authors also point out that the word *social,* in the term social entrepreneurs, simply modifies entrepreneurship, but the term still alludes to the concept of value creation conceived by Schumpeter (1997), who understands that the entrepreneur is an actor of change, inserted in a larger economy.

According to Oliveira (2003), social entrepreneurship is part of a paradoxical and complex reality. It stems from the decline in employment levels due to the rise in the value of self-employment, the advance of the globalization process, the search for capital and, at the same time, the progress of civil society organization towards the empowerment of social segments in peripheral regions.

Despite the paradoxical and complex reality, as defined by Oliveira (2003), the practice of social entrepreneurship by people fosters the creation of social values. This practice is based on innovating methodologies, providing services or manufacturing products capable of generating social change. In this way, people who practice entrepreneurship are called social entrepreneurs.

Referring to practitioners of social entrepreneurship, Bose (2012) points out that:

> Thus, the figure of the social entrepreneur emerged, as the leader capable of bringing together individual, private and collective resources to enable the development and implementation of solutions to chronic social problems (BOSE, 2012, p. 35).

The stance of the social entrepreneur conveys determinations characterized by the combination of social purpose, with an entrepreneurial spine, allied to the dynamic and innovative character of the business.

The idea of social entrepreneurship is associated with opportunities. It is therefore clear that when social entrepreneurs seize new opportunities, they make a commitment (which is the drive needed to continue) and stand firm to bear the risks inherent in the business.

Therefore, social entrepreneurship personalizes the business opportunity in the context in which it is located, according to the set of personal characteristics that the entrepreneur possesses, which are necessary to identify, pursue and create certain results from this opportunity.

According to Martin and Osberg (2007), entrepreneurs:

> are never fully compensated for the time, risks, effort and capital they spend on their ventures. We believe that the fundamental distinction between entrepreneurship and social entrepreneurship lies in the value proposition for you. (MARTIN; OSBERG, 2007, p. 34)

The social entrepreneur, however, does not anticipate or organize to create substantial financial profit for his investors, philanthropic and governmental organizations, or for himself. On the contrary, the social entrepreneur aims to generate value on a large scale, transforming it into a benefit for society.

The risks taken by social entrepreneurs can certainly generate income. What differentiates social entrepreneurship is the primacy of social benefit (as a mission), linked to the social impact it intends to have on society.

Unlike the corporate value proposition, which aims to reach a slice of the market that can afford to pay for innovation, the social entrepreneur's value proposition targets the part of society that is considered deprived, neglected or highly disadvantaged, and which does not have sufficient financial means or political influence to change its social reality on its own.

When aiming for social benefit, social entrepreneurs are driven by the identification of an injustice, which leads to the exclusion or marginalization of a social segment that lacks the financial resources or political influence to achieve any transformative benefit. For this reason, they develop proposals to generate social value by inspiring the creation of direct actions capable of bringing about change in the face of inert social problems. Finally, they generate, establish and stabilize a balance, capable of unleashing the potential of the social group. In this way, the generation of a stable context brings a new balance to the society involved in the social entrepreneurship network.

The incubation of social enterprises at the Padre Leo Association began in the 2000s, although the Association has existed since 1996. When companies join the incubator, they become members of a social network made up of actors who establish relationships of solidarity.

Social incubators are dedicated to encouraging social entrepreneurship: they support start-ups in developing products and services so that the activities of these new businesses can have a positive impact on society.

In relation to business incubation, Aerts; Matthyssens; Vandenbempt (2007) point out that they have played a role in stimulating entrepreneurship, as they are the breeding ground for talented entrepreneurs and leaders, capable of launching projects with a major economic and social impact, known as social enterprises.

For the EMES (Emergence of Social Enterprise in Europe) research network, an international reference on the subject, social enterprises are defined as organizations that explicitly aim to benefit the community. They are created by a group of citizens and where the return on investment made by investors is subject to limits, thus valuing independence and the reduction of economic risks related to socio-economic activities (EMES, 2016).

The term *social enterprise* emerged in the United States when non-governmental organizations began to expand their commercial activities. This movement was stimulated by the scarcity of resources generated by the retraction of state funding, which began at the end of the 1970s (KERLIN, 2006).

In the North American view of Kerlin (2006), it is notable that the term is understood as a way of encompassing organizations of various kinds involved in socially beneficial activities.

Still from a North American perspective, Dees (1998) notes that social enterprises are moving towards a market orientation as a way of maintaining their social activity and becoming less dependent on donations and grants, and more on fees and contracts.

According to the author, the reasons for this trend are: the development of capitalism and growing confidence in the power of competition and profit to promote efficiency and innovation; the promotion of social welfare without causing dependence on those who benefit; the search for more sustainable sources of funding (the development of activities that generate income seems to be more reliable than donations and subsidies); a change in the focus of institutions that allocate resources to non-profit organizations, as they prefer to foster companies with more commercial approaches; and the action of competitive forces (traditional and non-profit companies with a market orientation).

Regarding the work of social enterprises, Dees (1998) reveals a range of services they support, such as education, the arts, medical care, housing, combating hunger, environmental pollution, domestic violence and drug use. According to the author, they operate in areas where the market alone would not adequately meet the needs and/or complement government action.

In addition to the North American view, which understands social enterprises as private sector organizations that operate according to market logic with a focus on viable solutions to social problems, there is the Brazilian point of view on the concept of social enterprises.

Fischer and Comini (2012) present two perspectives on the concept of social enterprises. The European one, born from a tradition of social economy, such as associations and cooperatives, highlights the activities of civil society organizations with public functions. The predominant line of thought in developing countries emphasizes market initiatives aimed at reducing poverty and transforming the social conditions of marginalized or excluded individuals.

For Comini; Rosolen; Tiscoski (2014), social enterprises can be defined as: dual-purpose companies that adapt their profit goals to social objectives (hybrid); or non-profit organizations, committed to developing commercial activities that support the execution of their mission (social purpose organizations).

Thus, social enterprises are those that have a social purpose, i.e. their efforts are directed towards producing or offering services that benefit society.

By looking for an incubator, the social enterprise reduces a series of complex situations that it would experience if it weren't incubated, such as the lack of support in implementing new processes aimed at creating new products and services, little information offered by the entities that provide advice and difficulty in accessing information on raising financial resources. For Cunha (2013), the incubation process is usually where most of the group's learning and work takes place.

Incubators give the social enterprises they host the advantage of turning business ideas into real businesses, so that they can improve their competitiveness levels, germinate innovative companies with a high degree of positive social impact, and enter into partnerships with public authorities to sell their products and services, for example.

According to Cunha (2013), the work of the incubator includes some principles that need to be taken into account:

> the monitoring process is ongoing and takes place on *site* with all the incubated groups (weekly, whenever possible; the construction of demands and solutions to all the issues raised must be done together with the incubated groups, in a pedagogical proposal that is in line with Freirean methods; the protagonism of the venture's actors is a central element in the process, this does not mean that the team is not involved in the project's execution process, with all the support raised, however its role is more of a supporter and facilitator. (CUNHA, 2013, p. 20)

In addition to the learning aspects pointed out by Cunha (2013), the probability of failure of an incubated company is reduced when it belongs to a social network, as the actors promote cooperation strategies in order to develop the business initiative. Even though they have flexible or subsidized costs, they acquire administrative management skills over time.

The raison d'être of social incubators is to promote economic growth by giving disadvantaged people greater access to resources to set up their own businesses.

Since social entrepreneurs create and generate impact on the growth of the incubated business, they are the main actors contributing to its development.

2 THE ASSOCIATION FOR HUMAN PROMOTION AND THE RESCUE OF CITIZENSHIP FATHER LEO COMMISSARI

The Padre Leo Commissari Human Promotion and Citizenship Rescue Association, referred to in this work as the Padre Leo Commissari Association, was created and idealized by Father Leo Commissari in 1996, through a cooperation project between Italy and Brazil, called the Imola Sao Bernardo do Campo Solidarity Project, made up of Italian missionary priests. The aim of this project was to offer professional training that could contribute to people's individual development, as perceived by the increase in income from work, through a social network.

Also in 1996, shortly after the creation of the Padre Leo Association, the Padre Leo Commissari Vocational Training Center began offering training courses as part of the Imola Sao Bernardo do Campo Solidarity Project, in order to meet and adapt to regional needs for people's vocational training.

2.1 The Regional Context

Faced with the changes that took place in the world of work in the 1990s, unemployment in the region reached high levels, which required the Association to redesign the professional training it provided, as its graduates realized that the possibility of finding formal employment in companies was low, as the supply had practically disappeared. So the Professional Training Center began to inspire its students, in each of the courses offered, to become entrepreneurs, guiding them to set up their businesses in the Solidarity and Alternative Economy Network, called the "Commissari Network".

By characterizing the Montanhao neighbourhood, it will be possible to understand the regional context in which the Commissari Network and the Incubator of Solidarity Economic Enterprises (IEES) of the Padre Leo Commissari Association emerged.

2.1.1 Sao Bernardo do Campo

According to data from the Sao Bernardo do Campo City Hall, released in 2016, the city's population in 2015 was 816,925 inhabitants[1] , divided into 25 neighborhoods, including the Montanhao neighborhood.

The inhabitants of Sao Bernardo do Campo represent approximately 30% of the total population of the Greater ABC Paulista region[2] . This may reflect the fact that the city was one of Brazil's biggest industrial hubs when car manufacturers set up shop there in the 1950s, attracting workers interested in taking up the new jobs, who in turn took up residence in the city's 25 neighborhoods and have remained with their families to this day, especially in the Montanhao neighborhood.

2.1.2 The Montanhao neighborhood

The Montanhao neighborhood is a suburb of Sao Bernardo do Campo that had 84,515 inhabitants in 2000 and became home to 102,245 in 2015, i.e. 17.34% more people moved into the group of 30 villages and communities located among the hills belonging to the Serra do Mar mountain range that surround the city of Sao Bernardo do Campo. According to the

In Sao Bernardo do Campo, the population of the Montanhao neighborhood corresponds to 12.52% of the municipality's population[3] , with the largest number of inhabitants in the municipality of Sao Bernardo do Campo compared to the other neighborhoods, which calls for public policies and alternatives for generating work and income for the population.

Despite these social mishaps, Montanhao, according to Gattai (2013), is closely observed by organizations such as the Fernand Braudel Institute, in relation to the working realities of the neighborhood's inhabitants. In this sense, successful

---

[1] Available at < http://www.saobernardo.sp.gov.br/web/sbc/a-cidade-em-numeros>.
[2] IBGE estimate for the Grande ABC Paulista region, made up of seven cities: Santo Andre, Sao Bernardo, Sao Caetano do Sul, Diadema, Maua, Ribeirao Pires and Rio Grande da Serra.
Available at < http://www.saobernardo.sp.gov.br/web/sbc/a-cidade-em-numeros>.

experiences in the community point to local potential that stimulates the commercialization of products and services, so that the wealth remains in the community itself, such as the Padre Leo Commissari Human Promotion and Citizenship Rescue Association, which, in addition to offering professional training courses, acts as a business incubator and fosters a solidarity economy network, called the Commissari Network.

2.2 The Commissari Network

Rede Commissari is a solidarity economy network that creates personal and commercial relationships aimed at generating employment and income for people in the Montanhao neighborhood. Founded in 2002 on the initiative of the Padre Leo Association, the Commissari Network, through its leaders, dialogued with and invited entrepreneurs from the Montanhao neighborhood to join the social network, so that their respective connections and arrangements would facilitate commercial buying and selling relationships with customers who were interested in their products and services.

As a result of the dialogue that the Association had with people interested in joining the network, organized into cooperatives, its leaders realized that they would need to invest in another form of action that was within the entity's objectives, but which, due to a lack of human resources, had not been viable until now: the formation of cooperative groups.

In 2002, it set up an interdisciplinary team made up of five university graduates from the Methodist University of Sao Paulo (UMESP) and the Faculty of Industrial Engineering of the FEI University Center with the specific task of stimulating the formation and/or strengthening of alternative income generation groups within the principles of cooperativism and the solidarity economy. This interdisciplinary team was called the Solidarity Economy Support Group (GAES).

GAES played a role not only in inspiring the students at the Training Center to become entrepreneurs and set up their businesses on the Net, but also in encouraging the students to turn their thoughts and eyes to the real possibilities of generating income from transforming their ideas into businesses. GAES also made the students aware of the survival risks their business creations could face if they didn't know how to manage them.

GAES worked in a circular process. In the first stage, technical vocational training was offered and, simultaneously and interspersed, there were citizen training meetings, where realities were problematized, as well as their causes, needs and possibilities for changing them. Secondly, for those who wished to continue with entrepreneurial training, with a view to starting their own business or improving the one they already had, marketing and management training was offered[4] .

After this new professional training process, the student groups devised ways of organizing their businesses. GAES provided an administrative consultant who would accompany the creation and growth of businesses that wanted to connect to the Commissari Network.

From that moment on, the Commissari Network began to connect the region's entrepreneurs, graduates of the Vocational Training Center run by the Father Leo Commissari Association, with the network's players who began to act as customers for the products and services offered by the participating businesses. These customers included schools, nurseries, commercial establishments and individuals who became interested in the products and services marketed by the network.

Duly connected through the Commissari Network, the entrepreneurs began to plan the common benefits that could be achieved through collective and solidarity support and which could culminate in financial gains. Today, the Commissari Network has 17 ventures in the most varied fields of activity, as shown in Table 2, sorted in descending order of year of foundation and length of participation in the network.

Table 1 - Commissari Network ventures by time of participation, year of foundation and number of people involved

Source:<http://www.padreleo.org.br>. Accessed on August 7, 2016.

ENTERPRISE	LINE OF BUSINESS	YEAR FOUNDED	length of participation in the network (in years)	NUMBER OF PEOPLE INVOLVED
Sao Jorge Market and Winery	Food, drinks and cleaning products	1990	14 years old	2
Wind Cold	Clothing	1992	14 years old	7
Thie's Bar	Bar	1993	14 years old	7
My Kitchen Restaurant	Restaurant	1993	14 years old	2
Rich Auto Pegas	Sales of autoparts	1995	14 years old	6
Gomes Market	Food, drinks and cleaning products	1998	14 years old	3
Lued Bazaar	Bazaar and stationery	2000	14 years old	2
Yasmin's	Trims	2004	12 years old	4
Coopertativa de Trabalho dos Profissionais Operacionais do Sector de Construgao Civil (COOPROFIS)	Construction	2005	11 years	20
Grafica Nova Opgao	Graphic Services	2005	11 years	4
Helio Crystals	Glassworks	2005	11 years	3
Creative Apparel	Making	2006	10 years	6
Selecta Cooperative	Cleaning products manufacturer	2006	10 years	10
Deposit of Materials Matos Construction	Commercialization of building materials	2007	9 years	6
Art Cooperative Charlote Sewing	Bag and uniform making	2009	7 years	6
Company of Women	Bread, cakes and sweets manufacturer	2012	4 years	4
New Line	Joinery for the production and installation of planned furniture	2014	2 years	4

Source: author's own

There were entrepreneurs who already had their businesses before the network was set up, but also others who were motivated to set them up after the Commissari Network was conceived. Motivated by the principles of the solidarity economy, they saw in the idea of setting up their businesses opportunities to establish personal and commercial relationships aimed at generating work, so that their arrangements in the network would facilitate commercial buying and selling relationships with customers who were interested in their products and services.

In this context, three cooperatives were founded: the Selecta Cooperative (COOPER SELECTA), which manufactures soaps, disinfectants, pastes and other cleaning products, using used cooking oil as its main input; the Charlotte Art and Sewing Cooperative, which makes bags and uniforms; and the Work Cooperative for Professionals in the Civil Construction Sector (COOPROFIS), made up of bricklayers working in the civil construction sector. These ventures came about with the support of the Father Leo Commissari Association, which guided them through the processes of opening their businesses.

As a way of encouraging the Commissari Network to continue, the Padre Leo Association offered physical space on its land so that some enterprises could incubate their businesses. The Selecta Cooperative and the Charlotte Art and Sewing Cooperative accepted the premises provided by the Father Leo Association as support so that they could develop their activities. Other businesses asked for financial support from Italian organizations - Italian city halls and the Catholic Church - but only COOPROFIS, Deposito de Materiais de Construgao Matos and Helio Cristais got this kind of support to keep their businesses going and remained in the Commissari Network.

The creation of the Incubator of Solidarity Economic Enterprises was driven by the Padre Leo Association to support, strengthen and promote sustainable socio-economic development through the solidarity economy, as a strategy to combat unemployment and generate work and income for the people involved in the enterprises.

With the financial support it received, COOPROFIS rented its own physical space to set up the cooperative, but remained connected to the Commissari Network. With the money raised, it bought tools, personal protective equipment and uniforms so that, from then on, it could increase its customer base, which it aimed to integrate with individuals, companies and developers in the construction industry who needed professionals to carry out construction, renovations and repairs.

Some entrepreneurs gave up on joining the Commissari Network on the grounds that they hadn't received financial support from Italian organizations and felt that the physical space offered by the Padre Leo Association wouldn't meet the needs of their businesses; others went back to work for companies in the region and others kept their businesses going even without financial support and physically outside the Padre Leo Association, but remained connected to the Commissari Network.

Cooperativa Selecta and Cooperativa de Arte e Costura Charlotte accepted the proposal and were able to adapt their activities to the environment provided. Once Cooperativa Selecta and Cooperativa de Arte e Costura Charlotte had accepted Associagao Padre Leo's offer, they agreed that the maximum time each cooperative would remain in the incubator, from the time they joined until they left, should be around three years. The Father Leo Association and the cooperatives jointly understood that this would be enough time for them to acquire the administrative maturity to learn how to manage their businesses themselves, in a space outside the incubator.

The agreement signed by the Padre Leo Association with the incubated cooperatives consisted, among other things, of making them aware of the importance of being connected to the Commissari Network not only during the incubation period, but even after the end of the incubation period, so that the network would be strengthened.

As strategies to strengthen the Commissari Network, the Padre Leo Association, the main promoter of the network, signed a partnership with the Methodist University of Sao Paulo (UMESP), the Faculty of Industrial Engineering of the FEI University Center and the Bank of Brazil to form part of the GAES, in which each institutional partner had the intention of collaborating in a way to strengthen the network.

Through a three-year university extension project called Management and Service Networks for a Community of Solidarity, UMESP professors designed financial management and business management courses for the entrepreneurs taking part in the Commisari Network under the tutorship of the professors. This partnership was set up on a one-off basis to provide technical training for these entrepreneurs. The return on this project for the network has been an increase in learning for the entrepreneurs, who have improved their skills and abilities in entrepreneurial management, applicable to their respective businesses and areas of activity.

The participation of the Faculty of Industrial Engineering of the FEI University Center consisted of the work of teachers and students through a university extension project that would also last three years. The aim was to provide guidance and assistance to the entrepreneurs in planning their work processes in relation to the manufacture of each cooperative's products: Cooperativa Selecta (COOPER SELECTA), in the transformation of cooking oil into cleaning products such as soap, and Charlotte, in the manufacture of its bags and uniforms. This help has led to the entrepreneurs learning more about how to improve each of their production processes.

Banco do Brasil also established a partnership, which was limited to financially subsidizing the purchase of machinery and equipment needed to automate the production process of the Selecta Cooperative. The bank felt that it should only finance this cooperative because, compared to Charlotte, it did not have an automated production process, i.e. it carried out all the stages of manufacturing cleaning products, including soap, manually.

The FEI professors and students, who were also responsible for planning the manufacturing work processes for the Selecta Cooperative's products, consequently recommended to Banco do Brasil the types of machinery and equipment that should be purchased.

On the verge of ending the training process for the leaders of the Selecta Cooperative and the Charlotte Art and Sewing Cooperative, the GAES team, made up of people from UMESP and FEI, had a meeting with the leaders of the Padre Leo Commissari Association and put the following question on the agenda: "Should we end our support for the entrepreneurs in the network and let them survive and develop independently?". These partners had the common view, discussed several times between them, that their respective support was fundamental for training, advice and, consequently, for the strengthening and sustainability of the enterprises that made up the network. However, they knew that the cooperatives and the Commissari Network needed to become autonomous and that, after three years of working together, it was time to reflect on whether this network would continue to be alive and active without their presence and support.

GAES then decided, with the agreement and recognition of the leaders of the Padre Leo Commissari Association and the cooperatives incubated there, that the partnership needed to end, given the joint need for the businesses to become autonomous and collaborate so that the Commissari Network could continue and progress towards consolidation, since the incubator could provide the assistance that each business needed. However, the professors and students from UMESP and FEI pointed out that the cooperatives still needed the support of at least one business consultant. So the Padre Leo Association kept the same consultant it had hired until then, to continue to provide advice and support, both to the enterprises that were incubated and to those that would be joining the incubator.

In 2014, Charlotte left the incubator. This decision was taken by its leaders together with the consultant from the Father Leo Commissari Association, as they felt that the business had reached sufficient administrative maturity to manage itself outside the incubator, but remained connected to the Commissari Network. At this point, New Line, an enterprise focused on the manufacture of planned furniture, expressed its desire to incubate its business at the Father Leo Association and become part of the network, and was accepted.

Thus, the two businesses incubated at the Padre Leo Association and which are the targets of this work are: Selecta Cooperative, which transforms cooking oil into cleaning products, and New Line, which designs, manufactures and sells furniture.

2.2.1 The Selecta Cooperative

Since it was founded, the Selecta Cooperative has been making cleaning products such as liquid and bar soaps, shine pastes and detergents from cooking oils that have already been used in frying. The oils are collected by the cooperative's team of entrepreneurs, who go to homes, schools, snack bars, bars and restaurants in the Montanhao neighborhood, considered partners of the Commissari Network, who are already aware that incorrect disposal of cooking oil can cause damage to the environment, remove these cooking oils and take them to the cooperative's headquarters so that they can be transformed into cleaning products.

Once the cooking oils have arrived at the Selecta Cooperative, those that are fit to be used in the production process are selected, because if the oils collected have too many solid residues, they cannot be used, as the quality standard set for each cleaning product cannot be jeopardized.

The cleaning products manufactured by the Selecta Cooperative are sold to the chain's partners, who have given away their used cooking oil as a raw material. In this way, the cooperative is able to charge lower prices than those charged by large supermarket chains that are not part of the Commissari Network. This form of marketing can strengthen the businesses participating in the social network arrangement and increase their financial gains through their social relationships.

The Selecta Cooperative has been incubated for six years, although the time allotted for it to achieve self-management was three years. However, the consultant has provided effective support and reports monthly to the leaders of the Padre Leo Association on the stages of development and maturation that the business has reached. The biggest obstacles preventing the cooperative from becoming self-managing is obtaining authorization from the National Health Surveillance Agency (ANVISA), which recommends a physical space three times larger for the nature of the operation it is proposing, the manufacture of cleaning products.

This recommendation would become an obstacle, because the Padre Leo Association's incubator has limited physical space to that which Cooperativa Selecta currently occupies and leaving the incubator would mean the end of the incubation process and the beginning of self-management. The increase in physical space recommended by ANVISA, among other aspects, would imply significant changes in the production process, which would lead to an increase in costs, for which the consultant does not yet perceive maturity in entrepreneurial management.

2.2.2 New Line

New Line, founded at the beginning of 2014 and incubated since then, is a furniture manufacturing business that is also part of the Commissari Network. It is an entrepreneurial initiative in the carpentry industry, made up of four partners, one of whom is a designer, one a carpenter, one a salesperson and one an installer, since it is a business that designs, produces, sells and installs custom-made furniture requested by customers.

New Line customers can have their needs and desires met in relation to planned furniture by means of *software* used by the designer. This is a third-dimension simulation of environments configured according to the measurements taken of the environments to be organized and/or required by the clients.

The development serves several neighborhoods in Sao Bernardo do Campo and the city of Sao Paulo and greater Sao Paulo, as clients are attracted through the intermediary of the salesman, who visits houses and apartment complexes in the final stages of construction, geographically located outside the Montanhao neighborhood.

Despite the fact that they are different businesses and branches of activity, every two weeks, the consultant from the Padre Leo Association organizes groups of leaders from the two incubated businesses to discuss, propose and build the administrative support for each activity and organize their ways of acting as a network. A monthly contribution of R$10.00 plus (1%) of what is sold between the businesses in the Commissari Network is requested for the maintenance of the Association and its incubator.

Thus, with the collaboration of the cooperatives and businesses connected to it, by encouraging a fairer economy, the Commissari Network strives to build and strengthen socio-productive arrangements that are economically viable, ecologically sustainable and socially just through information, marketing and consumption of production, because the entrepreneurs who are part of it are organized in solidarity economic relationships to achieve development.

3 METHODOLOGY

This qualitative case study begins with a bibliographical survey that draws on theoretical bases to support the investigation, the aim of which is to analyze how the incubator of the Padre Leo Commissari Association promotes the development of incubated companies through articulation in the Commissari Network.

The first part of the bibliographic research was carried out by surveying the production of articles published in scientific journals, master's dissertations and doctoral theses, available on university websites and open repositories, thus forming the theoretical framework.

Next, data was collected from the Brazilian Institute of Geography and Statistics (IBGE), and from the Sao Bernardo do Campo City Hall Data Summary to characterize the municipality and the neighbourhood in which the social incubator is located. These are: population, age group and gender.

The research was based on two assumptions: firstly, that by becoming an incubator, each company would reduce the chances of suffering impacts that would be detrimental to its continuity, and secondly, that incubation would be an income-generating process for those involved in the New Line company - as a manufacturer of planned furniture - and the Selecta Cooperative - a cooperative that manufactures cleaning products. These assumptions allow us to verify the importance of the incubator in improving the living conditions of the people who work in both the New Line company and the Selecta Cooperative.

Only New Line and Cooperativa Selecta are resident in the incubator, in the process of being incubated. Interviews were therefore conducted with the members of both the Selecta Cooperative and the New Line company in order to understand the advantages of belonging to the Comissari Network.

There were 12 interviews, 8 from the Selecta Cooperative and 4 from the New Line company. These interviews were conducted using a semi-structured script (APPENDIX A).

In addition to the interviews with the directors of the Selecta Cooperative and the directors of the New Line company, an interview was also conducted with an employee of the Association, who monitors and advises on the administrative management of both incubated businesses.

All the interviews were scheduled by telephone and the purpose of the research was explained. All interviewees signed an Informed Consent Form (APPENDIX B).

The interviews were analyzed according to Minayo's (2001) proposal, which states that it is necessary to seek the respondents' understanding beyond the discourse and appearances of what is being communicated (MINAYO, 2001).

4 RESEARCH RESULTS

Initially, it will characterize the profile of the interviewees from each of the businesses incubated at the Padre Leo Commissari Association, the Selecta Cooperative and the New Line company. Secondly, it will identify the relationships that these professionals establish with the process of managing and developing the social networks inherent to each organization, as well as the reasons why they sought out the incubator.

The managers of New Line, a furniture manufacturer, are characterized in Table 3 according to their education and age.

Table 2 - Schooling by age at New Line

Schooling X Age	Complete elementary school	High School Completed
0 - 17 years		
18 - 29 years		
30 - 45 years	1	1
46 - 59 years		1
60 years or older		1

Source: research.

As for the Selecta Cooperative interviewees, Table 4, most of the directors have completed high school, similar to New Line.

Once the respondents have been characterized, we will try to analyze the content of the discourse with the leaders of Cooperativa Selecta and New Line, who will be identified in this analysis as follows: *Respondents* from Cooperativa Selecta will be identified by the capital letters A to H and those from New Line by the letters I to L.

First, the discourse of the leaders of the Selecta Cooperative will be analyzed. When asked why they sought out the social incubator, Respondent A said:

41

> The incubator plays this role for us: the steps we have to follow with regard to the production process and the administrative management of the Cooperative, because there are times when we have to make a decision here that we don't know where to start and it provides the help we need. (Respondent A, 25 years old).

Through the consultancy carried out by Father Leo Commissari, an employee of the association, the leaders of the Selecta Cooperative feel supported in their decision-making, not only with regard to price formation, revenue generation, costs and expenses, but especially with regard to the licenses required for the production and marketing of their products. One respondent said:

> I sought help from her incubator on things we didn't know. Because the Padre Leo Association had a consultant with more knowledge and a desire to help us, I saw that we could be helped here with environmental licenses. (Respondent H, 38 years old).

The speech of the respondent whose speech was transcribed above shows his concern about obtaining environmental licenses, which are fundamental to the operation of the business, and corroborates Respondent B, in relation to the advisory role that the consultant plays in the incubated businesses:

> We're nudging Ailton (consultant) every day, saying: we need this and we want this to have a solution. Let's go after it and find out where it's going, where we're going to look, who we're going to talk to." (Respondent B, 27 years old).

As the same consultant has accompanied the Selecta Cooperative since its creation and incubation process, the content analysis of Respondent B's discourse allows us to see that one of the cooperative's leaders recognizes his learning through the consultant's management guidance for the Selecta Cooperative. Related to this, Respondent F said:

> We don't want the incubator to do it for us. We want it to advise us on what we should do, who we should look for, or bring someone to tell us what we need to solve this or that. (Respondent F, 63 years old).

It's possible to see that the consultant's work has helped to raise the level of learning among the leaders of the Selecta Cooperative, as they reveal in their speeches. They are aware of the current needs of the business, including how to obtain a license from ANVISA so that they can produce and market on a larger scale.

> What we really want is for our products to be within the law, legalized, so that we can say: this is our business, where we can work and present our products. (Respondent D, 57 years old).

Respondent D also said that she "wanted help from the incubator", referring to obtaining licenses to reach more clients of the Commissari Network.

The position of Respondent C (61 years old) is similar to that of Respondent F, regarding her expectations of the incubator, when she says: "We don't want money from the incubator, we just want guidance". This attitude may be due to the fact that these respondents are married. This can interfere with relationships and perceptions of the business. This result may confirm Granovetter's (1973) conception of *strong bonds,* where the configuration of the social relationship comes from integration, cohesion and unity, capable of making the actors involved able to act in solidarity with reliability in their actions. In the case of Respondents C and F, in the light of the aforementioned author, the strong bond can be perceived, since there is proximity between the two, characterizing integration, cohesion and unity regarding their expectations of the incubator.

Respondent E (46) said:

> In addition to the incubator, the municipality could very well set us up in a place, in an unoccupied shed where we could produce, because here the

> physical space is insufficient to carry out the productive activities of our business. (Respondent E, 46 years old).

If we look at Respondent E's speech, we can see, albeit implicitly, that he is unhappy with the inadequate physical space that the Selecta Cooperative currently occupies in the incubator and believes that the municipality could provide another place for them to operate their production. However, their discourse makes no mention of the needs they still have for legalization with ANVISA, because if they were outside the incubator, they could lose the consultancy and liaison that the Padre Leo Association provides through the consultant.

When the leaders of the Selecta Cooperative were asked which social network they joined when they joined the social incubator of the Padre Leo Commissari Association, they replied that it was the Commissari Network. Respondent A explained:

> I've known about the Association for a long time, I even had the pleasure of living with Father Leo Commissari, the founder of the Association, and I know how concerned he was to give people knowledge so that they could change their lives. (Respondent F, 63 years old).

Respondent F's speech shows that the courses promoted by the Professional Training Center and the Commissari Network are the result of the founder's, Father Leo Commissari, concern for knowledge, which can change lives.

> We still don't have an income that you could say is worth it. But within all the knowledge, friendships, lakes of friendship, companionship, that have been created, that counts more than a big salary that I can have. (Respondent C, 61).

The change in life resulting from the connections established in the Commissari Network was understood by Respondent C from various perspectives, including: knowledge, lakes of friendship and companionship, but in the end he stated that these factors were more important than the large salary he could earn.

44

Regarding income, Respondent E acknowledged:

> One interesting thing that came up after we were incubated as a cooperative and were in the network, was that oil donation grew and we realized that we could also generate an income. (Respondent E, 46 years old).

Reiterating Respondent E's speech, Respondent A said: [...] I realize that the Association welcomes all those who have needs and want to pursue their goals, who seek knowledge. My life has changed in this sense. The good salary comes later, and we're moving towards that (Respondent A, 25 years old).

What Respondent A referred to was complemented by Respondent B, who detailed the trajectory of the leaders of the Selecta Cooperative:

> [...] Sometimes we get worried, thinking that we haven't made any progress, but we look back and see that we used to work only two days a week and today we work from 9am to 5pm ... Sometimes on Saturdays and Sundays we're at fairs, showing our work [...] This has been a very good change." (Respondent B, 27 years old).

Regarding the change in her life as a result of being part of the Commissari Network, Respondent G said:

> You can see the fruit of our work, everything we've built, in a network, that you can't find out there. Being invited to the Federal University of Sao Carlos and the University of Campinas to bring to university students the knowledge of someone who has never sat on a bench in a university and managed to do it and meet the needs of a group that needed to work, was very important. (Respondent G, 61).

When the leaders of Cooperativa Selecta were asked what their perception of the incubator was for the cooperative's maturation, Respondent A said:

> Outside we were unknown, inside the incubator we become better known. Talking about the Padre Leo Association is like talking about something welcoming, we know that people come here and find shelter." (Respondent A, 25 years old).

Respondent A's statement indicates his sense of belonging to the Padre Leo Association, in relation to the protection and solidarity provided by the social links established between people in the incubator. This corroborates what Respondent F said, comparing the fact of running a cooperative under the protection of the incubator with the possibility, according to the respondent, of being outside it: "If we were outside we would be very vulnerable, you know? Very much at the mercy of those who don't have the incubator's eye". (Respondent F, 63).

Respondent B reinforces Respondent F's statement about the protective nature of the Selecta Cooperative's operations when he said:

> [...] We only work and produce peacefully because we are protected here by the incubator. If we'd been outside, we'd have already paid a lot of fines or closed down, right? The Padre Leo Association is a mother, a protection, so that the cooperative can mature." (Respondent B, 27 years old).

Respondent H gave a different answer:

> [...] It's not interesting that we sell to the big markets when we have all the licengas, because they'll come in and say: we *want a huge quantity of cleaning products* and we'll work day and night, without a break to keep up; they won't pay a fair price. In the solidarity economy, the price needs to be fair, because in it, the human being is the protagonist of the story. (Respondent H, 38 years old).

Respondent H's statement shows that there is concern about environmental licenses and the future of Cooperativa Selecta's market in relation to its clients.

After analyzing the interviews with the leaders of the Selecta Cooperative, we tried to visualize the reasons why the respondents from the New Line company sought out the social incubator. Respondent I confessed to this:

> At first I didn't know it was a social incubator, I went in thinking it was a business incubator. I've had other businesses, and I think I've failed at some point and things haven't turned out the way I'd hoped. So I thought that joining an incubator was what I needed to avoid making the same mistake. (Respondent I, 43 years old).

What characterizes the Padre Leo Association as a social incubator are the aspects of participation and synergistic connections in solidarity economy networks, capable of developing and generating changes in the lives of the actors involved.

Regarding the search for the social incubator, Respondent J reported:

> [...] I had another activity before, I didn't think it was as profitable as I thought and I looked for another alternative, because I've always enjoyed working in this field, which is furniture, assembling custom-made furniture. (Respondent J, 39 years old).

Respondent J's account shows that the expectation of income and the affinity with the business of producing, assembling and fitting custom-made furniture prompted him to join the incubator.

Respondent K (47) stated that "in theory I don't depend on the income from here. I found the opportunity to become a partner in a business".

Respondent K's account, compared to the responses of the other New Line respondents, shows that although he says that "in theory" he doesn't depend on the income from the business, i.e. the payment of his pro-labour, the fact that he found the opportunity to become a partner presupposes a financial interest, focused on the expectation that the activity will be profitable.

Respondent L (60), also a member of New Line, replied that he was looking for someone in the social incubator: "someone who needed a manager, because if not, I wouldn't have come to this position at New Line".

When the members of New Line were asked which social network they joined when they joined the social incubator of the Father Leo Commissari Association, they replied that it was the Commissari Network. This question was complemented by a question about how being part of the Commissari Network had changed their lives. Respondent I said:

> Being on social media hasn't changed anything. Being in the incubator has. There's a lot of talk about this social network, but I don't see it. I don't know if it's because we serve another audience, which isn't this social network [...] That's bullshit [...] I don't help, they don't help me." (Respondent I, 43 years old).

Respondent I's comments differ from those of the leaders of the Selecta Cooperative: while the members of Selecta say that the Commissari Network has changed their lives, the same is true of the members of Newline, for whom the fact that their clients come from other neighborhoods, even outside Sao Bernardo do Campo, means that they are not integrated into the network.

The relationship that the New Line company has with Rede Commissari, relationships located in different places and with varying social relationships, are open relationships, i.e. they do not depend on the clientele and the product offered.

Respondent K has a similar view to Respondent I, when he said:

> I've been to a few meetings, so you're talking to the artisans from I don't know where, the popcorn makers [...] we're on a different track, man. It's not that way. The incubator is 10, but the network [...] (Respondent K, 47 years old).

The answer given by Respondent K leads to the perception that he doesn't see the importance of the network in changing people's lives, since there are connections between partners in a social network. The accounts of the leaders of the Selecta Cooperative show that they recognize the importance of this social network in their lives. Granoveter (1973) adds that:

> Individuals with few weak lakes would be deprived of information from distant parts of the social system and, as such, confined to the news and provincial views of their closest friends (GRANOVETTER, 1973, p. 1368).

Junqueira (2000) agrees with Granoveter (1973) that networks are built between autonomous social beings who share objectives that guide their actions and who respect the autonomy and differences of each member.

When the leaders of New Line were asked about their perception of the incubator for the maturation of the company, Respondent L said:

> Here we have an orientation that puts a brake on us. No matter how busy we are, there are frequent meetings to review everything we're doing and our plans for the future. I think that's one of the great advantages (Respondent L, 60).

According to Cunha (2013), the meetings that take place between leaders of organizations in the process of incubation are a central element, because in these meetings the construction of demands is conceived and the solutions to all the issues raised are made jointly. Analyzing this perception leads to the identification of one of the incubator's main roles, which is to support and facilitate business between those involved.

Respondent J, regarding his perception of the incubator for the maturation of the company, said:

> Here at the Padre Leo Association there's a whole range of information and interaction that I think is very rich, such as IT, mechanics, electricity, with the courses that are given here and always other heads thinking about other sectors here at Padre Leo. (Respondent J, 39).

Through the Professional Training Center, New Line members maintain connections with teachers and students, which allows for the exchange of knowledge and continuous learning.

Respondent I mentions having two alternatives:

> [...] open a small carpentry shop, in a garage, and start there, or join New Line, here in the incubator. I wanted to be part of a slightly different structure, so I wanted to join the incubator because as a company, in this field of activity, the customer notices greater security. (Repondent I, 43 years old).

Respondent I's statement about "greater security" may refer to the perception of guarantee and quality that the client can have when hiring the carpentry service of a company based in the incubator of the Padre Leo Association, compared to a small garage.

The fact that the monthly income of each leader of the Selecta Cooperative went from one third of the minimum wage[5] before the incubation to one third of the minimum wage after the incubation, allows us to infer that they attribute the change in their lives, expressed in the increase in their monthly income, to the Commissari o network. However, this does not mean that this increase was enough to remove them from a situation of social vulnerability, since the partners who work for New Line reported receiving salaries of R$2,000.00 each.

When asked what they were looking for in the social incubator, the consultant, characterized as Respondent M, said: "Since my arrival, at the time of GAES, I have tried to support the incubated businesses with my knowledge of management, because they lack this assistance."

When Respondent M was asked about his membership of the Father Leo

---

This is a minimum wage in force, set by the state government.

Association network, he said he joined the Commissari Network.

> the incubator has become a reference point for various situations... it provides management guidance services, obtains operating licenses and liaises politically with the Sao Bernardo do Campo City Council and the region. (Respondent M, 41 years old).

He added:

> [...] without the support of this structure, the leaders would find it difficult to take on such issues," especially the environmental education cooperative and the enterprise that produces and sells furniture (Respondent M, 41).

It was confirmed in the interview with Respondent M that he monitors the Selecta Cooperative and New Line on a weekly basis to ensure that the administrative management is being effective. By analyzing this aspect of the interview with the consultant, it is possible to agree with Cunha (2013) that there is a need for continuous follow-up with all the incubated groups to discuss the demands and solutions to the issues raised jointly with the groups. The recognition of the importance of this follow-up can be seen in the statements of some of the respondents, leaders of the Selecta Cooperative and partners of the New Line company.

The assumptions of this study are confirmed when we consider the speeches of the leaders of the units, i.e. that each company, by incubating itself, would reduce the chances of suffering impacts that would be detrimental to its continuity, and that incubation would be a process of income generation for the actors involved in the New Line company - as a manufacturer of planned furniture - and in the Selecta Cooperative - a cooperative that manufactures cleaning products. These assumptions allow us to verify the importance of the incubator in improving the living conditions of the people who work in both the New Line company and the Selecta Cooperative.

Finally, it was noted that one of the biggest difficulties facing the Selecta

Cooperative was the difficulty it would have in negotiating the necessary licenses to adapt its production activity. As an incubated cooperative, it relies on the interface of the Padre Leo Association, including administrative and political guidance.

5 FINAL CONSIDERATIONS

The study discussed how the process of social management and development takes place through networks and involvement in the solidarity economy social enterprises of the Padre Leo Commissari Association. The demand for the social incubator is due to the search for business security.

It was observed that the activities of each of the ventures helped to bring about social change and progress in the development of the businesses. This is evident in the significant increase in the entrepreneurs' income compared to the time before they joined the incubator.

Among the changes perceived, apart from the increase in the entrepreneurs' income, are the aspects of social management, which Fischer (2002) defines as the collective and participatory nature of the actors, whose contours are outlined in the social processes, power relations, conflicts and learning. Thus, the collective and participatory nature of the social management process can be seen in the actors' identification of social networks and the opportunities they have seen in them to make their companies thrive, even when they are incubated.

As for the social networks, it was concluded that the links established were important for the development of the incubated social enterprises, because it was clear that connections could be established between them and in the management processes. The integration of the social enterprises with the neighborhood which, in a cohesive and united manner, demonstrated solidarity and reliability in the actions.

The analysis of the research results led to the conclusion that development is the result of various interrelated actions and phenomena in a process between social actors positioned in their own space and time, and that the social incubator of the Padre Leo Commissari Association was the space of maturation, at least for the social enterprises that reside there.

It was concluded that the social incubator plays an important role in the entrepreneurs' learning process, since during the incubation period they acquire administrative management skills, so as to reduce the likelihood of bankruptcy when their ventures move on to the self-management phase, especially when they are supported by someone who acts as a consultant.

As a suggestion for future studies on the subject, we would highlight the need to study the possibility of incubated social entrepreneurs identifying the importance of belonging to social networks.

It is hoped that this research will contribute to the discussion on the subject of social management with the effective participation of citizens, proving that there are greater possibilities for social autonomy and development to be achieved through the active presence of the individual in the decisions that directly influence their lives.

REFERENCES

AERTS, K; MATTHYSSENS, P; VANDENBEMPT, K. **Critical role screening practices in European business incubators.** Technovation, n. 27, p. 254-267, 2007. Available at: <
https://businessmanagementphd.files.wordpress.Com/2014/11/aerts-et-al-2007- critical-role-and-screening-practices-of-european-incubators-technovation.pdf>.

Accessed on April 23, 2016.

ALCANTARA, F.H.C. **Municipal public policies and solidarity economy.** INTERAQOES, Campo Grande, v.15, n. 1, p. 135-145, Jan./Jun. 2014. Available at: <http://www.scielo.br/pdf/inter/v15n1/v15n1a13.pdf>. Accessed on 09 Apr. 2016.

BARCELOS, E. da S. **Autogestao: desafios politicos e metodologicos na incubagao de empreendimentos economicos solidarios.** Revista Katalysis, v. 11, n. 1, p. 96-104, Jan. / Jun. 2008. Available at: <
http://www.scielo.br/pdf/rk/v11n1/09.pdf>. Accessed on May 11, 2016.

BIRLEY, S. **The Role of Networks in the Entrepreneurial Process.** Journal of Business Venturing, v.1, p. 107-117, 1985.

BRANDAO, C. A. **Territorio & desenvolvimento: as multiplas entre o local e o global.** 2 ed. Campinas: Editora da Unicamp, 2012.

BOSE, M. **Social entrepreneurship and the promotion of local development**. Thesis (Doctorate in Administration). University of Sao Paulo, Sao Paulo, 2012. Available at: <http://www.teses.usp.br/teses/disponiveis/12/12139/tde-27032013-170655/en-br.php>. Accessed on 08 Apr. 2016.

CAILLE, A. **Sur les concepts d'economie en general et d'economie solidaire en particuliere**. La Revue du Mauss semestrielle, n. 21 (Alter-economie: quelle autre mondialisation?), Paris: La Decouverte, 2003.

CARDENAS, M. S. A; CASTANO, J. A. B. **Caracterizacion de unidades productivas associativas del programa de ecconomia solidaria de la Alcadia de Medellin**. Semestre Economico, Medellin, v.17, n. 36, p. 101-132, Jul./Dec. 2014. Available at: <http://www.scielo.org.co/pdf/seec/v17n36/v17n36a6.pdf>. Accessed on 09 Apr. 2016.

CARVALHO, M. C. B. Social management and public policies: an issue still under debate in the 21st century. *In:* JUNQUEIRA, L. A. P.; DIAS, S. L. F.G.; WANDERLEY, M. B.; MENDONQA, P. (eds.). **Social management: mobilizations and connections**. ENAPEGS Collection, vol. VI. Sao Paulo: LCTE Editora, 2013.

CARVALHO, M. C. B. Gestao social: alguns apontamentos para o debate. In: **Gestao social** - uma questão em debate. Sao Paulo: EDUC-IEE, 1999. p. 19-29.

CARRION, R.M. The contribution of social management to development. *In:* CANQADO, A. C.; TENORIO, F.G.; SILVA Jr, J.T.. (eds.). **Gestao social Aspectos Teoricos e Aplicagoes**. Colegao gestao e desenvolvimento, VI. Series. Ijui: Ed. Unijui, 2012.

CASTELLS, M. **A sociedade em Rede - a era da informação: Economia Sociedade e Cultura**. Sao Paulo: Paz e Terra, 2000.

COMINI G. M.; ROSOLEN, T.; TISCOSK, G. P. **Social Entrepreneurship and Social Business: A Bibliometric Study of National and International Publications**. Revista Interdisciplinar de Gestao Social, Salvador, v.3, n.1, p.85105, jan./ apr. 2014.

CORREA, V. S.; VALE, G. M. V. **Social networks, entrepreneurial profile and trajectories.** R. Adm, Sao Paulo, v. 49, n. 1, p. 77-88, Jan./Feb./Mar. 2014. Available at: <http://www.scielo.br/pdf/rausp/v49n1/a07v49n1.pdf>. Accessed on 09 Apr. 2016.

COSTA, I. **Social capital as an instrument for enabling local and sustainable development:** a comparative study of localities participating in the "new cariri" pact within the SEBRAE-PB / *REDE DLIS* program. 2007. Dissertation (Master's in Production Engineering). Federal University of Paraiba, Joao Pessoa.

CUNHA, E. V. Introducing the discussions: the Technological Incubator of Popular and Solidarity Enterprises (ITEPS) and its lessons learned in dialogue with other experiences. *In:* CUNHA, E. V. da; MEDEIROS, A. C.; TAVARES, A. de O. (eds.). **Incubation in Solidarity Economy: Reflections on its Practices and Methodologies.** Fortaleza: Imprece, 2013.

DEES, J. G. **Enterprising Nonprofits**. Harvard Business Review, v. 76, n. 1, p. 55, jan./feb. 1998. Available at: <http://go.galegroup.com/ps/i.do?id=GALE>. Accessed on: May 12, 2016

DOWBOR, L. Social reproduction. *In:* **Governability and decentralization.** Sao Paulo em Perspectiva, Fundapao Seade, vol. 10, n. 3, 1996, p. 21-31.

DOWBOR, L. KILSZTAJN, S. **Economia social no Brasil**. Sao Paulo: Editora Senac Sao Paulo, 2001.

EMES. **European Research Network**. Available at <http://www.emes.net/index.php?id=203>. Accessed on: May 11, 2016.

FERNANDES, F. **Mudanpas Sociais no Brasil**. Sao Paulo: European Book Diffusion, 1960.

FISCHER, R.M.; COMINI G. **Sustainable Development: From Responsibility to Entrepreneurship**. Revista de Administrapao da USP, Sao Paulo, v.47, n.3, p.363-369, jul./ago./set. 2012.

FISCHER, T. M. D. Local powers, development and management - an introduction to an agenda. *In:* FISCHER, T. M. D. (Org.) **Gestao do desenvolvimento e poderes locais:** marcos teoricos e avaliapao. Salvador: Casa da Qualidade, 2002. p. 12-32.
FISCHER, T. **Organizações e interorganizações na gestão do desenvolvimento socioterritorial**. Organizações e Sociedade, Salvador, v. 11, p. 13-41, 2004 (Special issue).

FISCHER, T. Territorial development as a field of convergence. *In:* JUNQUEIRA, L. A. P.; DIAS, S. L. F.G.; WANDERLEY, M. B.; MENDONQA, P. (eds.). **Social management: mobilizations and connections**. ENAPEGS Collection, vol. VI. Sao Paulo: LCTE Editora, 2013.

FRANQA FILHO, G. Social management between public administration and social work: a necessary dialog. *In:* JUNQUEIRA, L. A. P.; DIAS, S. L. F.G.; WANDERLEY, M. B.; MENDONQA, P. (eds.). **Social management: mobilizations and connections**. ENAPEGS Collection, vol. VI. Sao Paulo: LCTE Editora, 2013.

FRANCA FILHO, G. C. de; CUNHA, E. V. da. **Incubation of local solidarity economy**

networks: links and lessons learned from the experience of the Eco-Luzia project and the ITES/UFBA methodology. O&S - Salvador, v. 16, n. 51, p.725747, Oct./Dec. 2009. Available at:
<http://www.scielo.br/pdf/osoc/v16n51/07.pdf>. Accessed on: March 29, 2016.

FRANCA FILHO, G. C. de; LAVILLE, J.-L.; MEDEIROS, A. J. de S.; MAGNEN, J.-P. **Public Action and Solidarity Economy** - An International Perspective. Publisher: CIAGS/UFBA, Brazil, 2005.

FRANQA FILHO, G. C. de; LAVILLE, J.; MEDEIROS, A.; MAGNEN, J. P. (Orgs.). **Action publique et economie solidaire: une perspective internationale**. Toulouse: Eres, 2005.
FRANQA FILHO, G. C. de. **Theory and practice in solidarity economy: problems, challenges and vocation.** Civitas - Revista de Ciencias Sociais, Porto Alegre, v.7, n.1, p.155-174, Jan./Jun. 2007.

FRANCO, A. **Poverty & local development. Brasilia**: Brasilia, AED, 2002.

GASPAR PINTO, A. M.; JUNQUEIRA, L. A. P. **Power relations in a third sector network: a case study.** Revista de Administragao Publica, Rio de Janeiro, v.43, n.5, p.1091 -1116, Sept./Oct. 2009.

GATTAI, S. **The strengthening of the Montanhao solidarity economy network.** Revista Brasileira de Casos de Ensino em Administragao, Sao Paulo, v.3, n.2, p.01-09, Jul./Dec. 2013.

GATTAI, S.; BERNARDES, M. A. **Role and responsibilities of the university in the socio-educational process present in solidarity economy movements.** Revista de

Administragao Mackenzie, Sao Paulo, v.14, n.6, p.50-81, Nov./Dec. 2013.

GRANOVETTER, M. **Economic action and social structure: the problem of immersion.** RAE, v. 6, n. 1, art. 9, 2007. Available at: <http://rae.fgv.br/sites/rae.fgv.br/files/artigos/10.1590_S1676-56482007000100010.pdf>. Accessed on: 02 Feb. 2016.

GRANOVETTER, M. **The strength of weak ties.** American Journal of Sociology, v.78, n. 6, p. 1360-1380, 1973.
JUNQUEIRA, L. A. P. Social Management: Organization, Partnership and Social Networks. *In:* CANQADO, A. C., SILVA Jr., J. T. SCHOMMER, P. C., RIGO. A. **Os desafios da formagao em gestao social.** Palmas-To: Provisao, 2008 (p.87103).

JUNQUEIRA, L. A. P. **Intersectorality, transectorality and social networks in health.** Revista de Administragao Publica, v. 34, n. 6, p. 35-45, Nov./Dec. 2000. Available at: <http://bibliotecadigital.fgv.br/ojs/index.php/rap/article/viewFile/6346/4931>. Accessed on May 11, 2016.

KERLIN, J. **Social Enterprise in the United States and Europe: Understanding and Learning from the Differences.** Voluntas: International Journal of Voluntary and Nonprofit Organizations, v. 17, n. 3, p. 246-262, 2006. Available at: <http://dx.doi.org/10.1007/s11266-006-9016-2> Accessed on: May 11, 2016.

KRAMER, M. **Strategy and society: the link between competitive advantage and CSR.** Harvard Business Review, p. 52-66. Boston: HBS, Dec. 2006.

KRONEMBERGER, D. **Sustainable local development:** a practical approach. Sao Paulo: Editora Senac Sao Paulo, 2011.

LEAL, A. L. C. A.; FREITAS, A. A. F. de; COELHO, S. E. **The Perception of Opportunities in the Context of Social Entrepreneurship**. XXXVII ANPAD Meeting, Rio de Janeiro, p. 1-14, 2013. Available at < http://www.anpad.org.br/admin/pdf/2013_EnANPAD_ESO2061 .pdf>. Accessed on 09 Apr. 2016.

LOIOLA, E.; Lagemann, G. V. **Informal Social Networks of Incubated Companies.** Revista de Ciencias da Administragao, Joinville, v.15, n. 37, p. 2236, dec. 2013. Available at: <https://periodicos.ufsc.br/index.php/adm/article/view/2175-8077.2013v15n37p22/26100>. Accessed on April 9, 2016.

MAGRO, M.L.P.D.; COUTINHO, M.C. **Os sentidos do trabalho para sujeitos inseridos em empreendimentos solidarios**. Psicologia em Estudo, Maringa, v. 13, n. 4, p. 703-711, Oct./Dec. 2008.

MARTELETO, R. M.; SILVA, A. B. O. **Redes e Capital Social: o enfoque da informagao para o desenvolvimento local.** Ciencia da Informagao, Brasilia, v. 33, n. 3, p. 41-49, 2004.

MARTIN, R. L; OSBERG, S. **Social Entrepreneurship: The Case for Definition.** Stanford Social Innovation Review, Pallo Altto, v. 2, n.5, p. 27-39, 2007. Available at: <http://cddrl.fsi.stanford.edu/sites/default/files/2007SP_feature_martinosberg.pdf>. Accessed on April 25, 2016.

OFFREDI, C. Challenges and potential of social management in France and Brazil. *In:* JUNQUEIRA, L. A. P.; DIAS, S. L. F.G.; WANDERLEY, M. B.; MENDONQA, P. (eds.). **Social management: mobilizations and connections.** ENAPEGS Collection, vol. VI. Sao Paulo: LCTE Editora, 2013.

OLIVEIRA CORREA, R.; TEIXEIRA, R.M. **Entrepreneurial social networks for obtaining resources and organizational legitimacy: multiple case studies with social entrepreneurs.** RAM, Rev. Adm. Mackenzie, Sao Paulo, v.16, n. 1, p. 62-95, Jan./Feb. 2015. Available at: <
http://www.scielo.br/pdf/ram/v16n1/1518-6776-ram-16-01 -0062.pdf>. Accessed on 09 Apr. 2016.

OLIVEIRA, E. M. **Empreendedorismo social no Brasil: fundamentos e estrategias.** Franca, 2003. PhD thesis. Faculty of History, Law and Social Work - "Julio de Mesquita Filho" Paulista State University.

PARENTE, C.; COSTA, D.; SANTOS, M.; RITO CHAVES, R. **Social entrepreneurship: theoretical contributions to its definition.** XIV Encontro Nacional de Sociologia Industrial, das Organizações e do Trabalho Employment and social cohesion: from the regulatory crisis to the hegemony of globalization, Lisbon, p. 268-282, 2011. Available at <https://repositorio-aberto.up.pt/bitstream/10216/61862/2/cparenteempreendedorismo000151867.pd   f>. Accessed on 08 Apr. 2016.

PEYREFITTE, A. **The society of trust.** Rio de Janeiro: Topbooks, 1999. POLANYI, K. **Les systemes economiques**: dans l'histoire et dans l'economie. Paris: Librairie Larousse, 1975.

PORTER, M. **The competitive advantage of corporate philanthropy.** Harvard Business Review, p. 42-54. Boston: HBS, Dec. 2002.

RAICHELIS, R. **Articulation between public policy councils - an agenda to be tackled by civil society.** *In* Servigo Social e Sociedade, n. 85, p. 109-116. Sao Paulo: Cortez, Year XXVII, Mar. 2006.

RAICHELIS, R. **Democratizing the management of social policies - a challenge to be faced by civil society**. Revista Servigo Social e Saude: Formacao e Trabalho Profissional, v. 1, p. 1-17. Sao Paulo: Cortez, 1998.

RAICHELIS, R. **Esfera publica e conselhos de assistência social: caminhos da construção democratica**. Sao Paulo: Cortez, 1998.

RIBEIRO, S. D.; MUYLDER, C. F. de. **Solidarity Economy - In search of the essential elements of sustainability and solidarity.** Revista O&S, Salvador, v.21, n. 71, p. 581-614, Oct./Dec. 2014. Available at: <http://www.scielo.br/pdf/osoc/v21n71/1984-9230-osoc-21-71-00581.pdf>. Accessed on 09 Apr. 2016.

SACHS, Ignacy. Sustainable Development, decentralized bio-industrialization and new rural-urban configurations. The cases of India and Brazil. In: VIEIRA, P.F.E Weber, J. (eds). **Management of renewable natural resources and development: new challenges for environmental research**. Sao Paulo: Cortez, 1997.

SAMPAIO, C. A.C. Thinking about entrepreneurship from another rationality. *In:* JUNQUEIRA, L. A. P.; DIAS, S. L. F.G.; WANDERLEY, M. B.; MENDONQA, P. (eds.). **Social management: mobilizations and connections.** ENAPEGS Collection, vol. VI. Sao Paulo: LCTE Editora, 2013.

SANTOS, B.S. **The processes of globalization**. 2002. Available at: <http://www.eurozine.com/articles/2002-08-22-santos-pt.html>. Accessed on 04 Apr. 2016.
SCHUMPETER, J. A. **The theory of economic development**. Sao Paulo: Nova Cultural, 1997.

SEM, Amartya. **Development as freedom**. 1 ed. Sao Paulo: Editora Schwarcz, 1999.

SILVA, A. R. P. e.; BARBOSA, M. J. de S.; ALBUQUERQUE, F. dos S. **Sustentabilidade de empreendimentos econdmicos solidarios: analise da Cooperativa dos Fruticultores de Abaetetuba**. Revista de Administragao Publica, v. 47, n. 5, p. 1189-1211, Sept./Oct. 2013. Available at: <http://www.scielo.br/pdf/rap/v47n5/a06v47n5.pdf>. Accessed on May 11, 2016.

TENORIO, F.G. **Gestao social**: metodologia, casos e praticas. 5 ed. Rio de Janeiro: Editora FGV, 2007.

TENORIO, F.G. **Gestao social e gestao estrategica**: experiencias em desenvolvimento territorial. Rio de Janeiro: Editora FGV, 2013.

VALE, G.M.V. **Conditioning factors of entrepreneurship: social networks or social classes?** Organização & Sociedade, Salvador, v.22, n. 75, p. 583602, 2015. Available at: <http://scielo.br/pdf/osoc/v22n75/1413-585X-osoc-22- 75-0583.pdf>. Accessed on: 02 feb. 2016.

Printed by Books on Demand GmbH, Norderstedt / Germany